Red L...
&
Revelations

Jan Moran Neil

Indigo Dreams Publishing

First Edition: Red Lipstick & Revelations
First published in Great Britain in 2017 by:
Indigo Dreams Publishing
24 Forest Houses
Halwill
Beaworthy
EX21 5UU

www.indigodreams.co.uk

Jan Moran Neil has asserted her right under the Copyright, Designs and Patents Act 1988 to be identified as the author of this work.
©2017 Jan Moran Neil

ISBN 978-1-910834-24-4

British Library Cataloguing in Publication Data. A CIP record for this book can be obtained from the British Library.

Designed and typeset in Palatino Linotype by Indigo Dreams.
Cover design by Ronnie Goodyer at Indigo Dreams

Printed and bound in Great Britain by 4edge Ltd
www.4edge.co.uk

Papers used by Indigo Dreams are recyclable products made from wood grown in sustainable forests following the guidance of the Forest Stewardship Council.

For Syd, Jen, Jamie
and Ms xx Dannhauser who is due to reveal herself as we go to print.

Acknowledgements

I would like to thank my supervisor Professor Jem Poster at the University of Cambridge, the poet Patricia Sentinella and my husband Sydney Neil, who have all helped me to hear myself better.
And Dawn and Ronnie at Indigo Dreams Publishing.

Acknowledgements are also due to the editors of the following publications, in which some of these poems first appeared: Four Corners (Oxford University), Lunar Poetry, New Contrast SA, New London Writers, Reach, Rhyme & Reason, Royal Society of Literature Review, Sarasvati, South, World Wide Writers, Zoomorphic and other anthologies.

The South African based poems were recorded as part of a *Youth Empowerment Project* for Fruit-Nation NPC Masiphumelele, Cape Town and the poet can be heard reading on a Marlow FM Radio 97.5 interview which is available on www.janmoranneil.co.uk

Acknowledgement is made to Mrs C.H. Moore for 'We will talk it o'er together by and by.' taken from the hymn 'We are traveling home to Heaven by the straight and narrow way.'

Also by Jan Moran Neil

Blackberry Promises (novel)
Blackberry Promises, Brave Hearts & Baggage, The Deadly Factor (plays), New Theatre Publications, were performed on the London Fringe.
A President in Waiting ... performed at the Desmond Tutu HIV Youth Foundation Centre and Masambe, Baxter Theatre, Cape Town and for Cape Town TV.

CONTENTS

Red Lipstick
&
Revelations

Saving Grace

One night a bomb might go off
in Cardiff whilst you are in Shropshire
sitting on a sofa
not watching *MasterChef*
but you catch the shrapnel.

Or maybe there's a fire on the Jubilee line;
you missed the two twenty nine,
decided not to catch the exhibition
but a stationary cab with ticking meter instead.
Your wallet is in shock at Bond Street.

What if there had been a gas explosion
in Glasgow but you didn't complain
about your Benchmark Meeting
having been moved to Aberdeen?
You shiver.

Pull up your trench coat collar.
And tiptoe on.

God and Lipstick

My first day! My first client! Oh, my God.
And her completed form tells me she's eighty seven.
I'm giving her Bubble Bliss Heaven. Number
sixteen massage on the Client Care List. I say, 'I hope
you have a lovely stay. Is your lipstick
Max Factor? Or X Factor? Let's make a start then.'

She lies on the bed, all quiet like, and then
I'm thinking, it's like stroking a post mortem, dear God.
I say, 'You're wearing such a pretty lipstick.
And why not? Just a number, isn't it, eighty seven?
You've done well to get to that age. I hope
I get to that age. Head up a little. Yes, just a number.'

Then she croaks, 'Shall I tell you a story about a number?'
And I say, 'Oh, I love a story. Go on then.'
And then she says, 'It's a Story of Hope.
It's a Story of how I wish to meet God.
It's a Story about not just being eighty seven.
It's a Story about a Consignment of Lipstick.

'In the days of release they gifted us lipstick
and to us it meant we weren't just a number.
My number was A, two, six, one, eight, seven.
I had been a number, you see, up until then.
We were women who had never seen our faces or God
for years. We had forsaken hope.

'That ruby red stick gave us not food but hope.
We were just hollow women wearing lipstick.
I couldn't be sure, you see, there was a God
or if there was, was I to Him just a number?
I had been a number, you see, up until then.
I was A, two, six, one, eight, seven.

'And now I'm eighty seven.
And I've learned to make friends with hope.
It gave a female corpse the thought that then
she might meet God with a slash of lipstick
on her sealed mouth. A mouth with a number
and no name. Just Lipstick and God.'

It's then I notice it. Oh. My. God.
She's in Room Seven. The VIP Gold Star Suite's number.
Hope she won't report me for mentioning her lipstick.

Friday Night Fairy Tale

She first tried to speak to him in broken Quebecois.
Then, when he said his name was Israel,
she realised he wasn't French Canadian after all.
She swam in during the warm Fall, before the snow fell
on the eyebrow arches of her French Portuguese
Rue de Bullion appartement and at its mouth
there he stood, lightly bearded, clutching a bunch of keys.
A pardoned Nixon draftee, fighting his way
back to the lights of off-off Broadway, he sculpted
until dawn in the downstairs studio
with his pet rabbit Harvey, which she would never see.
On Fridays he collected rents for his papa.
Eventually, she became the final call
so they could feast on her fish rissoles and Chardonnay
whilst he ignored the unsheltered light bulbs,
the fractured lavatory cistern and the leaking water bed.
The slim cuisine swelling with shrimp and Gauloise fug,
they spoke of Vietnam, Biblical Ishmael and Isaac, dads,
whale blubber in lipstick and one wish granted
every Friday night to the court of the Crimson King,
Black Sabbath but sometimes Judy Collins,
wondering which butt end would be the last.
Syllables dribbled towards dawn with such importance.
They were like blind pianists
touching minims, fumbling in the white light
for the right keys to tap and that perfect fifth.
When snow drifted on to sills of the windows,
she knew he would leave stuffed into his Afghan coat.

But he didn't. She did.

And now across the ocean, she fancies
that he stripped, gutted and boned
the innards of that two storey appartement,

pulled apart the arteries, made it one clean whole,
sculpting her in monumental alabaster
in Montreal. Where he lives still,
with a frozen smile,
grieving.

Sealed in Table Bay

They are undecided.
Yellowtail or Kingklip?
The descending darkness speaks
of cooked fish
and her *Ginsberg is GOD*
eau de parfum
when suddenly she says,
'Is that a bin bag or a seal?'

On the tarmac where the jetty
forks into the Atlantic
dried fur wrestles;
a tower of tourists trickles by;
mobiles snip.
'The bull is sick,' he says.
'Someone should call for care.
It may be dead.'

Salt sits on the air.
They stare down, aloft, adrift.
'No,' she says. 'He is raising his head.
He just won't perform.'
Much later he calls the waitress
scribbling the perfumed air
signing for the bill.
The fluorescent lighting strip splutters.

'Is the seal ill?' she asks.
The caramel coloured girl replies,
'He not die. He come here to chill.'

The customer is satisfied.

It's hard to see the bin bag now;
black on black tarmac.
'Perhaps we should do it,' says she.
He says, 'Perhaps not.'

Drawing Board

It's 1962. Croydon.
I'm eight,
sitting next to Susan
tracing the Cape of Good Hope.

Our hands smell of carbolic soap
and I've got big plans.

Susan's tracing the toe of Africa
with her new wax crayons.
She won't share and I'm fed up with her
because she got ten out of ten for Reading Aloud.

My ocean's green and I'm sticking in some clouds.
And I've got big plans.

Susan's dad was a window cleaner
and she has shiny, new, patent black shoes
because her dad fell off a ladder
and the court gave compensation for being dead.

I'm using my dad's British Rail biros instead
and I've got big plans.

I'm planning to go to the foot of Africa
but Susan says my plans are bigger
than the Africa on my sugar paper
and I never will.

She thinks she knows it all does Susan Nashville.
But I've got big plans.

Fifty years on
and we winter in Cape Town .

My daughter calls and happens to be in Croydon.
She's in court pleading for the prosecution.

Yeh to my big plans.

And my small heart swells
as huge as that green Indian ocean.
But the bigger one seeps guilt as well
for eight year old Susan.

Saving Face

Washed ashore, swords passing through her,
stretchered on a table of sand,
she dreams of that other land,
where she swam with strips of cuttlefish.
Her protective tail, once supple scaled,
promised three hundred collagen
filled years and eternal oestrogen
resting ultimately
on a carpet of silver foam sea.

But she wanted infinity.

Lost her identity, voice, cadences,
questioning brow,
in exchange for a sea shell.
At first the needle, syringe,
then knife for new skin
to dance, dance, dance and dance again
in pain, on the bleeding waves.

For him?

Shipwrecked

You might be forgiven
for thinking this house is afloat,
Cape winds smashing against
port holes on a boat,
rain thundering inside
my sea blue ocean of a heart
which bleeds debris,
is floored,
cannot be moored,
will give no warning
if it is forced to clam up.

You might be forgiven
for thinking this house is afloat.
But it's not.

My hopeful feet to the south,
salt in my mouth,
and above my addled brain to the north
sleeps Africa dark dry and hot.

Tomorrow
you might be forgiven.
Tonight you are not.

Bored Husband

Your husband has just called
to say you can buy anything in this shop
the plaque reads.

But my husband stares out to sea;
examines the mainsails of catamarans
whilst I study the *Just Cruisin'*
swimwear.

We know everything in life
carries a price tag.

Amongst the bric-a-brac
there is another plaque which reads
Bored Husband.

I turn to check the price tag.
On the flip side reads ...
Not for Sale.

For Sale. Baby Girl. No name.
PO Box 61

Silver Surfing

So quite suddenly I Google your name.
And there you are. Whisper of what you were.
Oh, how I want you back again the same.
Not bald and at odds with the camera.
This is not the face that lives in my head.
Or the boy who surfed distant, dazzling seas.
No. This is what I would have had instead:
a faded photocopy creased like me.
Two spools of thought cannot be reconciled:
the past that glides, the one that's on this screen.
Whichever way both images are lined
with my not knowing the one in between.
Inadequate pixels and lines that flow
show nothing of my ebb. I let it go.

Dolly Pop and the Garage Wall

When Busisiwe said,
'You in red error and paid me
twenty rand less last Tuesday.'

When I asked Busisiwe,
'Where is my halter neck top?'
And she said, 'It be a mix up.'

When my throat erupted
and I said, 'Busisiwe, Busisiwe,
I'm no longer speaking to my sister.'

That was when she took my hand
across the gear stick, 'Your *only* sister,'
she said. (Busisiwe has seven.)

When I had to explain
that in my poem I used her sister's name
because 'Busisiwe' didn't rhyme.

When today she told me of Dolly Pop,
shot by police in a vigilante cross fire
and I said, 'I bought her Clearasil.'

That was when we made one black and white
nine-knuckled fist for Dolly Pop,
(Busisiwe has no little finger).

When Busisiwe said, 'Dolly Pop was twenty-six,
pregnant and partner-less,
and my nephew is only five.'

When we face the whitewashed wall,
suspended in No-Woman's Land,
still holding hands …

until I release the central locking
and Busisiwe, on alert, gets out,
picks up the shirts and once again
we are madam and maid.

White Rhino in Winter

And suddenly ... clamped on road side,
zooless, but ours for the viewing,
prehistoric pedestrian, pavement slab for hide,
blank blinkers stare seemingly, at nothing.

Handicapped horn bent towards winter earth,
the haunting whisper of captivated guide,
'She carried two calves for fourteen months.
She lost them last week to a pride.'

Mother's eyes on sun-drenched winter evening.
Weighted monument in mourning.

Magoo

A touch of the tar's a very base hue.
They slept without bars, no gun by the bed
but they always lived in fear of Magoo.

They reared sheep and owned a big white house too.
At Oudtshoorn their ancestral seed was spread.
A touch of the tar's a very base hue.

They housed Hottentot maids in the Karoo
and made sure their stock and children were fed
but they always lived in fear of Magoo.

The kids moved to Cape Town for something new,
stopped rearing sheep, entered banking instead.
A touch of the tar's a very base hue.

Guard dogs and razor wire rip guts right through
intruders who could creep into their bed.
Still, they always live in fear of Magoo.

They check the new-born's fingernails for blue
clasping their own hands in prayer and dread,
 a touch of the tar's a very base hue
fearing the bloodline of Ouma Magoo.

Maid to Clean

Tuesday:
I am discussing the sins and merits
of central heating
and The Welfare State
with Busisiwe
who is blissfully unaware of both
as she glides
from room to hollow swallow's room
lifting a banana skin
from my outstretched palm
this snow-capped spring September afternoon.

Wednesday:
Cousin/ brother Zwei has died
in a drunken brawl
leaving no funeral policy.
Her father's text request:
The three most responsible cousin sisters
who clean, to please make considerable
financial contribution.
I ask if Zwei at twenty seven will go to heaven.
Her reply:
'No. He was loved but he was very, very rude.'

Thursday:
Goat will be slaughtered for sacrifice
just as she and her six sisters all born in September
(father is home in December)
had their baby little fingers cut
and placed on the roof of the hut.
We sip coffee, stare through burglar bars.
Busisiwe considers. 'What are all those
little fingers doing on hut roofs?'
I say I don't know

but I will write a poem for Zwei.

I pick up my pen.
Busisiwe smiles mildly,
picks up her broom
and sweeps into the next room.

Intruders

We find them in the mornings,
dead under the sills,
not knowing how they have arrived
and search for cracks or holes.
Flying ants; it must be the weather
or something we have done.

We find them in the mornings,
pushed under the slit at our front door:
Birnam Wood to Dunsinane:
flies by some other name with glossy manes
advertising a cruise or new hair salons
where we can spend our pensions.

We find them in the mornings,
sleeking across our screens
begging bank details, screaming alerts.
We flick them, vacuum, press delete,
mouthing an inner curse.
They stain our silence.

And even in the evenings
silk-edged with soft rain
they come and come again
down the telephone line.
We are confused. How do they get in?
To our home: ordered, white, edited, pristine.

The Ballad of Ek en Jy

Roosenbosch African night air
Was spiced with the tang of wine;
The voorman sat on his bricked stoep
And surveyed the blossoming vine.

As he smoked his long-stemmed clay pipe
The South Easter caressed his lips,
Touched the mouth of his wyn vaatjie,
Whispering seductive gossip.

That wind could slice apart vineyards
Or cool the sun-drenched soul,
But this year the grapes were dripping
And the soil was darkly fertile.

This year had brought better pastures,
Coloured oxen driven to plough
Which yielded crops not castrated;
Now he thought only of the girl.

Paler than her Hottentot sisters,
She was harvest golden in hue,
Her silky pores enticed him,
Murmuring, 'Johann, me and you.'

Spread on the floor of his outhouse,
She whispered, 'Ek en Jy.'
The Afrikaans' God was silent,
'We'll be mit mekaar 'till we die.'

The seed was planted forever,
Fingernails would be searched for blue.
But this now is the back story
Of the voorman and his Magoo.

Bird Brains

We wonder what they think:
this gaggle of guinea fowl,
siren alarms of the dawn
en famille
stabbing through their bunched lavender.

We wonder what they think:
those leopard toads
stretching akimbo
through winter weeks
in their unchlorinated pool of green.

The yellow speckled
Christmas butterflies
flirting with the leaves
on their lemon tree.

The chaffinches that strike
the crust that's been stuck
to their razor wire
by brunching garden boys.

What do they think?

When two swallows
alight after breezy pause
with bags of noisy syllables
and drills
and bleating mobile phones
and gas cylinders
for braais

and outdoor living.

Stitched Up

I know a woman down Mitchells Plain.
She made bags for not much gain.
Night and day her fingers pain.
She had stitches on the brain.
She went here and she went there.
For snatch of rand she'd go anywhere.
Her bags so good people stop and stare.
Go search the market and compare.
She have a thread for a kangaroo.
She have a thread for Winnie the Pooh.
She make best threads for the Big Five.
Man, she brought those bags alive.
All the ladies who are white
They say these bags are cheap and light.
Then one day comes this woman called Jane.
She says, 'Bag Lady. You is insane.
I can sell these bags for much more gain.
Let me take some for the plane.'
Jane, she makes five times the bucks.
She gives Bag Lady a slice of the cut.
Then Jane asks, 'Bag Lady how you cut the grain?'
Bag Lady she happy to explain.
Then Jane set up shop in the UK.
Jane set up shops called BAGS BY JANE.
Bag Lady say, 'But that ain't my name.'
Jane says, 'Bag Lady I don't need you no more.'
Jane got girls stitching on factory floors.
Jane's selling fast in fancy stores.
JANE'S BAGS is facing price wars.
Now this woman down Mitchells Plain
She got no rand to catch the train.
Every time she try sell her bags
White women say, 'No Designer Tag.'

Birds in the Hand

At Africa's toe, black birds, come, it's time.
Arise from Khayelitsha, Gugulethu
and all those townships. Arise now and go
from shacks to big white houses down the line.
And catch the train from Mitchells Plain at five,
spill out from stations as South Easters blow,
click IsiXhosa, scatter then to brows
of hills and False Bay valleys to arrive
at eight, to clean plates, mind babas, sweep stoeps,
iron, fold it, get fed bread, pick up rand,
collect cast-off garments: re-invent them
to meet your own ends. Then you S-shaped, looped
starlings, fly, fly, slow gait back to shacks and
at dawn, arise and do it all again.

Hand in Glove

Pulling over on to the hard shoulder,
dipping the rear view mirror,
I catch your hand moulded in leather,
lying on the back seat of my Mazda.

An imprint of your palm and fingers coated
in a patina of winking headlights.
I was on my way, without you, to Strathclyde,
when all along, behind, were inches of your outline.

The cast is giving an unlikely thumbs up.
I recall you had a tentacle grip.
Now loosened and released I am left
not knowing if I am all right or bereft.

You gave me sixpence when I gifted you those gloves.
Soppy superstition: that one might lose a love,
travel in diverse directions, if they weren't paid for.
That unworn opal cost you far more.

We made a good pair when we met,
but you forced my hand to separate.
It's fitting that you are now behind;
the road ahead is long but wide.

The Undressing

Hair, hair, hair and hair, falling hair,
fleecing, hour by hour, sliced to the floor
and the crawling floor lives in my dream time;
can never betray the scissors that saved
me or the blade which met the skulled scalp:
my point of scratched contact. Now gone.

Gone, gone, gone and gone, long gone:
gone are the grim women, their scared hair;
gone the colour that springs from the scalp;
shaved sharp from the neckline, strand to the floor.
They are already undressed and nothing could save
them. Me. I was simply marking time.

Time, time, before the war there was time
to trim men's beards but now that's gone.
Long ago, boychiks' locks were keepsakes saved
to remind men as they grew bald of hair
they possessed before they grew old. Now, heil floor,
meet the final layer of who girls were. Scalped.

The finishing line is now blocked at the scalp.
Before the war I tapered the neckline, took time
as hair dropped to the black-white checked floor.
But now my shop – that has all gone
and all I have left here is the hair.
But then again it's the hair that has me saved.

Then they came in. I couldn't save
them. I touched their scalps.
I touched their hair.
I gave them time.
I slowly cut until it was all gone.
Until all their hair had fallen to the floor.

My wife. My daughter, bubbee. I looked at the floor.
When they saw me they thought they were saved.
Even when their hair had all gone,
when I could see their skulls beneath scalps.
Even then they thought they had time.
Now all that is of them is their hair.

Now in my dream time I scour the floor.
I don't see their scalps, but search for their hair.
Black locks. White locks. I couldn't save them. Gone.

Smoke Screen

We both wear wigs.
But at the end of the day
hers will be taken away.
I know.
Several sexual partners
account for bank deposits
of huge amounts of cash,
then again it's
not just hash but
Class A Drugs: cocaine;
six and a half kilos
vacuum- packed in the lining
of her lesbian lover's luggage.
'Corrupt Caribbean bag handlers,'
she has told me. 'Plants.'

For now she re-applies lilac lippy,
her green nails unfortunately chipped
and bloodied at her dark cuticles.
'Divine Pine by Jessica Nails.' She smiles.
I do not need to know this.

'You must remain within the confines
of the court,' the judge has said.
I do not say, 'This is not a good sign.'
But knowing today is not one to abstain, I inform her,
'You can smoke outside.'

Her eyeliner opens wide.
'I don't smoke.'

'Toshelle. You *told* me you smoke.'
She points a Divine Pine sideways
and mouths, 'My. Mother. Is. Here.'

Mother sits square-lipped, squat and resolute.

The judge sentences Toshelle to ten years.
There are tears.
There are always tears.

Stashing away my wig and gown
I tell Mum I can take her note down.

I always check the notes.
In the robing room.

Mother writes:
God does not sleep.
I know you are innocent.

Diminishing Returns

I remember taking less
and a little less
stuffing the gap in my gut
with the gap in the words
that were not being served
at the table
where I measured the spoons
for the paying guests
in the room that was shrouded
by conifer trees
and my eyes never cried
but were onions dried and then fried
with my bones as brittle as cracked egg shell,
my breath someone said was over boiled yolk,
my throat sounded like artichoke
so I took a little less
because it was all so hectic
and I overheard cousin Derek say,
'She might be dyslexic,'
but I knew I could read
and that Derek was as thick
as my chunky hips,
so I receded, concealed and never ever
revealed how I was shrinking my shrunk
because it wasn't worth it:
the growing of tits or the monthly pain,
the disposal of stale-smelling napkins,
so when they released me
to go on French Exchange
the pain au chocolat was devoured
with my eyes and not my mouth,
'cos I tasted in my head
and they said, *Elle mange comme un oiseau,*
little sparrow, little sparrow,

and when I flew back I remember
my mother wailed, 'Where did she go?'
and taking a little less and a little less
but I never remembered being little
just a big fat mess;
then I remember in the shopping arcade,
a boy saying, 'Look at that bird,
she's dead thin.'

And I'm thinking now, I could have been.
Anorexia. It's one long non-bleeding sentence.

Dressed to Kill

A sleek navy fit
flying over the hips
that uncrushable crepe de Chine.

It smelled of wood burning smoke
and it left her for broke
but it was indestructible crepe de Chine.

It lived in pilot-packed bars
where she sang to the stars
and she wore it the night she met him.

Pulled pints in it, kissed in it,
free fell and fibbed in it,
it might have been stitched up with wings.

Summers flew by in it,
did more than she should in it.
Well, it was just one of those things.

But when the neckline sagged
it had to be bagged
and had nowhere to go but the bin

along with the soldier who matched her blue,
a bottle of Estée Lauder *Youth Dew*
and that guilt-sodden night of sin.

Lip Service

Today we have discussed the depths
of John, Chapter Eight.
Knitted together
and cardiganed to the collar
we are pleased
with our hermetically sealed
jars of clotted jam
which sits, both sweet and tart
on bran bread, sliding
easily from our tongues
as our conversation slips smoothly
from Christian liturgy to female clergy

and those vicars who wear lipstick
and those members of the same sex
who hold hands,
those who demand the right to die,
Muslims who might not get to heaven.

We move from our homespun fudge
to consider Verse Seven
over peppermint tea rims
and our bias binding.
Let him without sin
be the first to cast a stone.

And so we sit with our bread
and even a little wine,
snug in the cushioned cellars of our souls.

Bread Pudding Days

On soggy days
when the rain spits
my mother's house is filled
with the warmth of cinnamon sticks,
rich dried fruit
and softly sifted sugar.
She folds and wraps our words:
the bargain cost of my orange gloves,
the price we paid for our lost loves,
our woeful tales of wicked hate,
our splendid plans to be great.
All are measured, sieved, considered
for their mixed worth
baked into something sturdy,
crusty, spongy and deeply palatable.

And in that cooking fragrance,
the weight and varied textures
touching half remembered edges,
my mother's syllables and smiles stretch on:
a balm against the greying bits,
a refuge against the rain which spits.

Stranraer

Dawn yawns.
My plump feet on platform four where
porters swoop,
gulls beckon.
London nightmares forgotten.

Ferry flurry
for Larne crossing
and the smell of morning
spreads like salty butter
on ten o'clock soda bread.

Old summers live on
in my giddy head.

Lines of Symmetry

Crisp, white envelopes.
Today I receive
Two sets of test results.
Cold instruments bring
Clinical returns,
As my finger bleeds on opening
Sharp edges.

Twice I read:

Your vagina is not giving correct information ...
Rejection: cervically-smeared nurses write.

Disappear into your womb for creation. **Rejection**:
Razor-nosed professors snipe.
Disappear into your womb for creation. **Rejection:**

Rejection: cervically-smeared nurses write.
Your vagina is not giving correct information ...

Twice I read:

Sharp edges.
As my finger bleeds on opening
Clinical returns,
Cold instruments bring
Two sets of test results.
Today I receive
Crisp, white envelopes.

brandon luvs sharleen

hi
hi
me M - u?
me F - 10
u cum here off 10?
ya – u how old?
13
y u luv sharleen?
she talks about her goals
she footballer?
wots footballer ? I live broncs
cool I live liverpool. footballer plays with balls
u mean she plays around
ya ....u still there? i wait yonks
ya my friend cs sharleen he gets attentive with sharleen i can only get
attentive with sharleen on internet
ic sad y u no life get? ....u still there brandon from
broncs?
ya u c me 2nite?
u got private jet?
cool sharleen is cool but u r lush ....u still there june from liverpool?
june?
june? i luv u june from liverpool brandon luvs june
brandon u r doomed

Death of an Actress
(acknowledging Louis MacNeice's poem of the same name)

I see from the internet that Lizzie Lyons is dead.
She was fifty six and her Facebook Page
states all that ever needs to be said:
She was a good actress, quite a loss to the stage.

She was once very close to becoming well known,
supported some 'A List' celebrity names;
she even penned some scripts of her own
that were sassy, surreal but otherwise tame.

She took one to Edinburgh in seventy eight
costing thousands of pounds and some bits of her hair.
The reviews all said it was a promising start
but after that it never really went anywhere.

Lizzie was inundated with 'Walk On 1' parts:
a barmaid, a stripper, that was her mark
and once she had three lines in a soap
which paid rent on her bedsit at Finsbury Park.

I looked up to Lizzie even though she was short,
understudying me in Shakespeare's *'Dream'*,
learning all the lines for nothing at all:
could never have passed as the Fairy Queen.

Then at one of the tributes I halted my cursor:
Trooper – wish that witch had let you go on.
You so would have made a better Titania.
Have always adored you. Your Oberon x

Scent for You ...

I will leave you some day
mid-sentence
with a *Calvin Klein Eternity* spray
barely begun,
half way through
a Bobbi Brown concealer
a moth-balled gown
a stamped letter never sent
a dress kept for Sunday Best
an uncorked Reserve Shiraz
an optimistic tote bag still bearing its tag
a scratchy scent of my syllables
on a cassette
somewhere in a drawer
found on a day far flung from here
with only these words left,
stopping mid-

Aunts and Feathers

I had aunts oozing
from every corner,
alighting from Cunard liners
like queens:
chignoned, high-heeled,
G-eyed avifauna.

Moulting mink,
they transmigrated my years:
a flock of honey blonde legs
and lips. Lips
which twitched
and pursed and sometimes cursed:
a chorus in cashmere,
telling tales as heady
as the straight scotch they sipped.
'Mu, it's not *what* you know,
it's *who* you know,'
in hats askew
which lifted without breeze.

They were something
towards which I could grow:
my mother's sisters,
and did I learn to mimic
their pearl-studded plumage
and those lifelong flights
in the Fall across the pond
importing all brands
of transatlantic baggage?

And thus my aunts
like my poems
stiletto on and on ...

a rare breed this,
now extinct,
for today I heard
the last one had gone ...

Grave Concerns

Quiet as 'A Quakers' Meeting':
that game we used to play;
just the squelch of my boots
on soft snow
freshly falling
on forever and forever fond farewells.

Dumb wombs facing east;
never giving birth,
married to the earth,
neighbours in adjoining rooms;
labelled with sweet sentiments
iced with kindness.

Letters of the alphabet,
deliberated then discarded,
resurrected now incarcerated,
the final gift,
signed off, templated
and set in granite.

My mother's thumbnail
points upwards, her details,
extra five pounds for a digit plus VAT,
shrouded in this sudden throw of snow,
I scrape away with a blue J Cloth
and feel her say

in a voice, at thirty eight when we met
or is it seventy seven when she was failing?

Look at that poor cow's grave next to me.
Not a soul to visit.
Not one papier-mâché poinsettia.
Give it a shovel with your trowel, love.

My mother.
She always gave me work to do.

Nature Calls

See, all my life, my work's been Death.
Lifelong undertaking's been our pride.
Son's a stone mason, wife's a dab hand with paint,
and I've buried more bodies in this 'ere yard
than your young 'un there has seen in her life.
Oh God, yes, burying, burying, now that's an art.

But ma'am, if you want to view Art,
lookey see how the Romanies mark Death.
Over yonder their head stones are larger than life.
Oh, yes, gypsies spend the greatest of pride
when they end their travels in the grave yard.
The wife says she never spares on *their* paint.

Some need more and some need less paint.
Embalming, heavens, now that's a skilled art.
Almost there, love, don't urinate in the yard.
Remember Lllewellyn who bludgeoned his kids to Death?
Well, they're all in there, the whole of his pride.
Him as well? No, missus, not on your life!

Myfanwy Lloyd took her own life.
Your mother's grave could take a lick of paint.
Now here's our card, we're known as The Cardiff Pride.
My son adds bell ringing to his fine art.
'Professionals in All Aspects of Death.'
Public conveniences top of yard.

Shipman lies in an unknown yard.
Meanest looking corpse I've seen in my life.
And I buried countless souls he sent to their Death.
My wife doctored them, bless 'em, with her paint.
That's an open can of worms and my art
is keeping discreet, that's me, Haydn Pride.

Now ... here lies Aunt Rhiannon Pride.
She, Lord love her, is the special in the yard.
Now Aunt Rhiannon's self-discipline was *her* art.
Watched her weight and was unlined all her life.
Aunt Rhiannon knew how to use war paint
but even she needed assistance at Death.

Rhiannon in Death would have been her pride.
Oh yes, best paint on a corpse in the yard.
Here's to the Ladies and my wife's life's art.

Bountiful Spring Buck:
Ballerinas of the Bush.
Tomorrow's breakfast.

Duty Free

She scarfs
the Yves St Laurent counter
with boarding pass
and enquires, 'Mascara?'
The male sales assistant
with eyes like sultanas
examines hers,
saying, *'Faux Cils,*
in Baby Blue, Purple
or how about Dramatic Black?'

She consults the rack.

'Shocking. The New Range.'
He half smiles. 'Make a change.'
Shiny, shimmering,
packaged and gold,
she knows what she is being sold.
She is unsure especially
when he recommends
'A New Wand.
Baby Blue for your grey eyes.'
Tannoy.

She complies.

Dashing for Departure Gate,
she's late.
Perhaps she should have opted
for Dramatic Black,
as stretching out on the tarmac
is A Life Beyond.

She's sixty,
she's duty free,
and clutching her wand.

The Next Stop

Daffodils at Dollis Hill are blooming,
he bundled up his bones in Belsize Park.
His heart in Redhill once needed pruning;
buried his senses in Barking after dark.
Bulbs of him got planted in Swiss Cottage,
they deadheaded his brain in Peckham Rye.
His head at Hanger Lane germinated;
at Seven Sisters they preserved his eye.
Bits of him are growing in the out shed;
his soul might be grafting in Crouch End.
Is he now rightly part of the undead
even though his blood and breath are now stemmed?
Daffodils at Dollis Hill are blooming;
but he was hardy and still keeps moving.

Feedback

Mother Hyena:
clearing agent of the veld,
stripper of white bones;
powdered faeces, false penis,
howling, hunchbacked editor.

God and Dolly Pop

Then I says, 'God,
now I'm here with no Clearasil
what you gonna do about my pockmarked skin?'

And God say, 'Dolly Pop,
your skin over here gonna be
as smooth as Baby Bottom Butter
you buy in Pick and Pay. Understood?'

And I say, 'Yes, Sir, God.
Are you from the US of A?'

And God say, 'If you like, Dolly Pop.
I'm gonna give you a smooth ride
and we gonna fly way high over Hollywood
and see all them stars I made.
I'm gonna be your personal pilot.'

And God's letters thread together like
violet Tanzanite on string slivers of silver.

Then I say, 'God, the words that come off your lips,
they shine. What shade are they?'

And God, She say, 'Dolly Pop,
the shade of my lipstick don't even exist yit.'

Chapter and Verse

Twenty years after Ma passed on,
we heaved down her Family Bible
on a tea time whim and therein discovered
our Cissie's christening certificate
in Genesis.

Lizzie married a Catholic mick.
Her confirmation card lurked in Leviticus Five
wedged under the biblical header 'For Ignorance'.

Excitement soared when, sandwiched
between Kings and Chronicles,
we spied saving coupons eligible for redemption.
We squirreled them away.

Christopher, of course, was clasped in sepia,
buried within Psalms under 'God's Protection'.
'He looked like lavender when he was laid out,
did our Christopher,' Cissie said. Then added,
'Blue eyed boy.'

We examined the Axminster.

In Memoriam cuttings were sprinkled
through chapter and verse:
'Dearly beloved brother George Pepper.
We will talk it o'er together by and by.'

We rabbited on
questioning the meaning of it all
as Ma's marriage licence fell
randomly from Lamentations.

Seek and ye shall find deliberately clipped
and on the flip side a model for a Herschel travel coat
'sweeping from shoulder to hip'.
This giant storage unit yielded
Ma's chronological trip.

Nosing on, we knew the answer
would lie in Revelation …

Indigo Dreams Publishing Ltd
24, Forest Houses
Cookworthy Moor
Halwill
Beaworthy
Devon
EX21 5UU
www.indigodreams.co.